D1415047

How Our
Government
Works

# What Does a
# SENATOR Do?

David J. Jakubiak

PowerKiDS
press™

New York

*To the Berroa family, thank you*

Published in 2010 by The Rosen Publishing Group, Inc.
29 East 21st Street, New York, NY 10010

First Edition

Editor: Amelie von Zumbusch
Book Design: Julio Gil
Photo Researcher: Jessica Gerweck

Photo Credits: Cover, p. 13 Ryan Kelly/Congressional Quarterly/Getty Images; pp. 5, 17 Scott J. Ferrell/ Congressional Quarterly/Getty Images; p. 6 Alex Wong/Getty Images; p. 9 Andy Nelson/The Christian Science Monitor via Getty Images; p. 10 Chip Somodevilla/Getty Images; p. 14 Martin H. Simon-Pool/ Getty Images; p. 18 Shutterstock.com; p. 21 Hank Walker/Time & Life Pictures/Getty Images.

Library of Congress Cataloging-in-Publication Data

Jakubiak, David J.
 What does a senator do? / David J. Jakubiak. — 1st ed.
    p. cm. — (How our government works)
 Includes index.
 ISBN 978-1-4358-9360-3 (library binding) — ISBN 978-1-4358-9816-5 (pbk.) —
 ISBN 978-1-4358-9817-2 (6-pack)
 1. Legislators—United States—Juvenile literature. 2. United States. Congress. Senate—Juvenile literature. 3. United States—Politics and government—Juvenile literature. I. Title.
 JK1276.J35 2010
 328.73'071—dc22
                          2009030931

Manufactured in the United States of America

CPSIA Compliance Information: Batch #WW10PK: For Further Information contact Rosen Publishing, New York, New York at 1-800-237-9932

# CONTENTS

# WHERE LAWS ARE MADE

In 1972, Congress wanted to stop water pollution. President Richard Nixon thought it would cost too much to do this. Then, Senator Edmund Muskie, of Maine, went to the Senate floor. He asked, "Can we afford clean water? . . . Can we afford life itself?. . . These questions answer themselves." Other senators agreed with him. Congress passed the **Clean Water Act** over the president's objection.

Laws start as bills in the Senate or the **House of Representatives**, the two houses of Congress. The Senate is made up of two senators from each state. Senators write laws and approve, or authorize, the president's picks for key jobs.

In 2009, senators such as Jeff Bingaman (front left), of New Mexico, and Chris Dodd (center), of Connecticut, tried to find ways to make health care less costly.

Senate majority leader Harry Reid (center) and minority leader Mitch McConnell (right) worked together to pass a bill to keep businesses running in 2009.

# THE RULES OF THE SENATE

When the U.S. government was set up, people considered using **population** to decide how many people each state sent to Congress. However, the leaders of small states feared that this plan meant they would go unheard. They reached a **compromise** with the people from larger states. The number of representatives from each state is based on population, but every state gets two senators.

Each **political party** has a Senate leader. The **minority** leader heads the party with fewer senators. The **majority** leader sets what the Senate will work on each day. Both leaders decide which senators will talk about which bills.

# BECOMING A SENATOR

Senators can come from many other jobs. Some started out in state government, while others worked in business. Actors or sports stars have been elected senators, too. Ohio even had an **astronaut** as a senator! In 1962, John Glenn became the first American to orbit, or circle, Earth. In 1974, Ohioans elected him to the Senate. Glenn served until 1999.

To be a senator from a state, you have to live in that state and be at least 30 years old. Senators serve six-year **terms**. Elections for the Senate take place every other year, with about one-third of the Senate up for election at a time.

People who run for the Senate must campaign, or make their case to voters. Here, Tennessee's Bob Corker (front left) is campaigning to become a senator.

Here, members of the Senate Judiciary Committee answer reporters' questions. One of this committee's jobs is to hold hearings on people who were picked to be judges.

# DOWN IN COMMITTEE

After a senator introduces a bill, it is sent to a group of senators called a committee. There, senators work on bills. Senators can add things to bills or take things out of bills. They can also let bills die. After a committee finishes with a bill, it is sent back to the full Senate.

The Senate has 20 committees. Each committee works on one subject. For example, the Senate Appropriations Committee directs how money is spent.

In 2004, Senator Thad Cochran, of Mississippi, wrote a bill to make school lunches healthier. The Senate Agriculture, Nutrition, and Forestry Committee worked on the bill. Congress passed the bill and President George W. Bush signed it into law.

# DEBATING ON THE SENATE FLOOR

In 1983, an argument exploded among senators over making Martin Luther King Jr.'s birthday a national holiday. Some argued that we should have a day to honor this American hero. Others said that giving people a day off would be too costly. The bill passed by a 78 to 20 vote. We now observe Martin Luther King Day on January 19 each year.

Senators can **debate** a bill before voting on it. During a debate, senators can talk only about the bill being considered. They must not say anything bad about other senators.

Senators can filibuster bills. In a filibuster, senators keep debating the bill instead of allowing a vote. A filibuster can be ended if 60 senators vote to force a vote on a bill.

Each year, senators debate the president's budget, or plan to spend money. In 2009, South Dakota senator John Thune (right) argued that the budget was too costly.

In 2009, President Barack Obama (seated) signed the Edward M. Kennedy Serve America Act. Kennedy (right) was a senator from Massachusetts.

# FROM A BILL TO A LAW

If the Senate and the House of Representatives both vote for a bill, it goes to the president. If the president signs a bill, it becomes law. However, if the president vetoes, or decides not to sign, it, that bill has one more chance. If the bill wins the votes of two-thirds of the people in both houses, it becomes law.

It often takes several months for a bill to become a law. Senator John E. Sununu, of New Hampshire, offered a bill calling for presidential dollar coins in May 2005. On December 22, 2005, President George W. Bush signed the bill. Today, those coins are being made.

# VOTING ON THE PRESIDENT'S CHOICES

In 2006, President George W. Bush chose Samuel Alito to fill an opening on the **Supreme Court**. Some senators wanted to filibuster to keep Alito off of the Court. They failed to do that and the Senate voted 72 to 25 to end debate. The next day, a 52 to 48 vote put Alito on the Supreme Court.

The vice president is officially the president of the Senate. However, vice presidents rarely come to the Senate. They generally vote in the Senate only to break a tie.

Along with passing laws, senators authorize picks the president makes for key jobs. The Senate approves Supreme Court justices and the head of the **Federal Bureau of Investigation** (FBI). Senators also vote on treaties, or agreements the president makes with other countries.

The Senate approved Michael Hayden (left) as the head of the Central Intelligence Agency (CIA) in 2006. Here, Hayden meets with Senator Olympia Snowe, of Maine.

Visitors to the U.S. Capitol, seen here, can take a tour of the building. They can even sit in on a Senate debate and hear senators arguing over important matters.

# WHERE THE SENATE WORKS

The Senate meets in the Capitol building, in Washington, D.C. On September 18, 1793, President George Washington laid the cornerstone of the Capitol. Since then, the building has had many changes. British troops set it on fire in 1814. In 1851, two new wings were added for the growing houses of Congress.

Not all the Senate's business is done at the Capitol. There is also space for offices for all 100 senators and several committees in the Russell Senate Office Building, the Dirksen Senate Office Building, and the Hart Senate Office Building. A subway for senators runs between these buildings and the Capitol.

# GREAT SENATE LEADERS

Throughout history, the Senate has offered a stage to powerful leaders. Presidents Barack Obama, John F. Kennedy, and Warren G. Harding all went from the Senate to the White House.

Others have used the Senate to change America. Senator Henry Cabot Lodge, of Massachusetts, backed moves to make the United States an independent world power. Senators Howard Baker, of Tennessee, and Edmund Muskie, of Maine, worked to keep air and water clean. Senator J. William Fulbright, of Arkansas, created a program that lets American students study in other countries, while students from other countries study in the United States.

John F. Kennedy served as a senator from Massachusetts from 1953 until 1960. In the Senate, Kennedy backed laws that helped workers.

# HARDWORKING SENATORS

Senators have also done important work in recent years. Senator Olympia Snowe, of Maine, has helped older Americans afford **medicine**. Senator Ted Kennedy, of Massachusetts, wrote laws to improve education and limit hunger. Senator Barbara Boxer, of California, has fought to clean up pollution and to keep drinking water safe. Senator Lindsey Graham, of South Carolina, introduced bills to aid military families.

Do you know who your senators are and what they are working on? If you do not, visit the Senate Web site to find out. Read about your senators and discover what they are doing in Washington, D.C.

# GLOSSARY

**astronaut** (AS-truh-not)  A person who is trained to travel in outer space.

**Clean Water Act** (KLEEN WAW-ter AKT)  A law that keeps water clean and safe.

**compromise** (KOM-pruh-myz)  An agreement in which both sides give something up.

**debate** (dih-BAYT)  To argue.

**Federal Bureau of Investigation** (FEH-deh-rul BYUHR-oh UV in-ves-tuh-GAY-shun)  A branch of the U.S. government that looks into crimes.

**House of Representatives** (HOWS UV reh-prih-ZEN-tuh-tivs)  A part of Congress, the law-making body of the U.S. government.

**majority** (muh-JOR-ih-tee)  Having the larger number.

**medicine** (MEH-duh-sin)  A drug that a doctor gives to fight illness.

**minority** (my-NOR-ih-tee)  Having to do with the smaller part of a group or a whole.

**political party** (puh-LIH-tih-kul PAR-tee)  A group of people that has similar beliefs in how the government affairs should be run.

**population** (pop-yoo-LAY-shun)  The number of people living in an area.

**Supreme Court** (suh-PREEM KORT)  The highest court in the United States.

**terms** (TURMZ)  Periods of time that elected officials can serve.

# INDEX

# WEB SITES

Due to the changing nature of Internet links, PowerKids Press has developed an online list of Web sites related to the subject of this book. This site is updated regularly. Please use this link to access the list: www.powerkidslinks.com/hogw/senator/